THE JOAN SUTHERLAND ALBUM

THE JOAN SUTHERLAND

A L B U M

Compiled by
JOAN SUTHERLAND
with
RICHARD BONYNGE

SIMON AND SCHUSTER
New York

Title page photograph: The rain couldn't stop Richard and
me from sightseeing in Venice, 1960

Published by Simon and Schuster
A division of Simon & Schuster, Inc.
Simon & Schuster Building
Rockefeller Center
1230 Avenue of the Americas
New York, New York 10020

Originally published in Australia by Craftsman House,
a division of The Craftsman's Press Pty. Limited
SIMON AND SCHUSTER and colophon are registered
trademarks of Simon & Schuster, Inc.

Designed by Judy Hungerford and Pamela Brewster
Printed and bound by Kyodo Printing Co. Ltd., Singapore

1 2 3 4 5 6 7 8 9 10

Library of Congress Cataloging-in-Publication Data

Sutherland, Joan, 1926–
The Joan Sutherland album.

Originally published: Australia: Craftsman House.
1. Sutherland, Joan, 1926–   . — Iconography.
2. Singers — Iconography.   I. Bonynge, Richard.
II. Title.
ML88.S95A3   1986   782.1'092'4 [B]   86-3961
ISBN 0-671-62669-8

CONTENTS

Luciano Pavarotti

April 4, 1986

I can barely remember my career without
Joan Sutherland. From the beginning when
she did invite me to Australia, I learned
from this special lady and extraordinary
singer so many things about the voice, the
stage and the career. It seems to me that
we have always been together on the stage
and that is truly what I like.

Luciano Pavarotti

FOREWORD

In assembling this collection of photographs, my problem was what not to include. I discovered boxes full which Joan and I had completely forgotten about and sometimes had difficulty in identifying. However, as the sole purpose of putting this album together was to give pleasure to one who has herself given so much pleasure to the world, I found only a little difficulty in rejecting certain pictures which she actively disliked. Then my publisher pointed out to me that unless I wanted to run into two tomes I would have to jettison another few hundred. Well, I shall doubtless return to the attack in ten years' time with the next instalment!

It seems an age since the late 1940s when we were both young and beginning our careers. We accomplished far more than we ever dreamed about or even hoped, but we have forgotten so much and lost so many pictorial memories. I can find none of the photographs which were taken of Joan with Lily Pons, Jeanette MacDonald, Ninon Vallin, Gladys Swarthout, Evelyn Laye, Eugene Goossens, Merle Oberon, Rock Hudson, Dame Edith Evans or Ingrid Bergman. But from a long and honourable career (which is not yet quite over) I have found enough to illustrate the story of a merry dance on four continents. Of course we are proud of what we have accomplished and have only very few regrets. It would have been nice for Joan to have performed *Don Pasquale* and *Thais* in the theatre but somehow they got left behind.

As for the direction of Joan's career, I believe it was the right one. Certainly to be singing rôles in such operas as *Norma, Lucia di Lammermoor, I Puritani, La Fille du Régiment* and *Anna Bolena* in one's sixtieth year in the world's major theatres says something, and after almost forty years of public performing. We have worked together for those forty years and been married for thirty-two of them. We have had a few good fights privately but have kept a united front in our dealings with theatres — I dare say we have sometimes given them a few headaches, but only because we believed thoroughly in what we were trying to do. Managements might have been happier had the repertoire included *Bohèmes, Toscas*, et. al., but we would have been less happy. We have enjoyed reviving lost eighteenth and nineteenth century masterpieces of bel canto and the French romantic repertoire, not to mention grubbing around in 'the ragbags of the nineteenth century' as some critic charmingly put it.

During our long careers many things have changed radically in the theatre and seldom for the better. Voices were on the whole bigger and better and techniques were stronger. Certainly in the 1940s, '50s and '60s there were far more star performers than there are today — and not only in the operatic world but in the ballet and straight theatre as well. There was far more sense of occasion in our early days — we miss the great galas when the audiences were bejewelled in magnificent gowns — these gala nights at La Scala, the Teatro Colon and the Opéra are sadly gone. Today they even come to the opera in T-shirts, shorts and thongs but I suppose the important thing is that they come.

We grew up a long way from the musical centres of the world but even so were lucky enough to have heard Richard Tauber, Georges Thill, Marjorie Lawrence, the great pianists Ignaz Friedman and Percy Grainger, and to have heard many concerts conducted by Otto Klemperer when he was young and Eugene Goossens. On our arrival in Europe we were in time to see Flagstad in all her final Wagner performances, Margherita Grandi, Margherita Carosio, Gigli, Schipa and the great pianists Gieseking, Edwin Fischer, Cortot and Lipatti. In her early days at Covent Garden, Joan sang with such legendary singers as the Konetzni sisters, Gottlob Frick, Hans Hotter, Stignani and Callas. We saw Toscanini, de Sabata and Stravinsky and Joan sang with Clemens Kraus, Erich Kleiber, Sir John Barbirolli and Fritz Stiedry — these are links with the beginning of this century.

Our operatic beginnings were not auspicious. In Sydney during the second world war there was practically no opera — a few performances at the Conservatorium (I began by coaching *Figaro* and *Falstaff*) and two visits from a touring Italian company playing the usual repertoire. We enjoyed performances by Rina Malatrasi, Mercedes Fortunati and Germana di Giulio, and soon found the way up the back stairs without paying so we could go every night. Of course we listened to records a lot in those pre-television days. Melba, Tetrazzini, Galli-Curci and Flagstad, Caruso, Martinelli and Tibbett were our favourites. Otherwise it was musical comedy and films. Gladys Moncrieff was our great star and we saw her and loved her in *The Merry Widow, Katinka* and *The Maid of the Mountains*. Many of the D'Oyly Carte company were stranded in Australia during the war and we heard Ivan Menzies and Evelyn Gardner in almost the entire Gilbert and Sullivan repertoire, over and over. At the films we adored Jeanette MacDonald, Miliza Korjus (who later became a very dear friend), Ilona Massey, Jan Kiepura and Marta Eggerth — the last two we saw on the stage in *The Merry Widow* in London. These were strong influences and only this year (1986) we had enormous fun recording many of the songs from the films of the 1930s, '40s and '50s — Joan remembers all the tunes.

We cut our balletic teeth on the Ballets Russes de Monte Carlo with the then baby ballerinas Toumanova, Riabouchinska and Baronova as well as the company of Helena Kirsova and Edouard Borovansky. In London we arrived at the right moment to see the beginnings of Festival Ballet and visits by the Danish Ballet, the Paris Opéra Ballet, the Ballet des Champs Elysées, Marquis de Cuevas, Ballet Theatre, New York City Ballet, Pilar Lopez, Josè Greco, et. al. We devoured the lot.

When we weren't at the ballet or the opera we went to the plays and saw so many great performances by Edith Evans, Sybil Thorndike, Edwige Feuillère, Olivier and Gielgud; and other nights we went to recitals by Josephine Baker, Charles Aznavour, Lena Horne and Yves Montand — we were like sponges and wanted to see and hear everything.

In our travels we often claimed that all we saw was the airport, the hotel and the concert hall. But happily this was not always true. On our trip to the Teatro Colon, Buenos Aires, we took ten days to visit La Paz in Bolivia and Lima, Cuzco and Machu Picchu in Peru. While in Tokyo we spent time by the sea and in Kyoto; from Barcelona we tripped around north-eastern Spain. We have had great trips to the Rockies, Yellowstone Park and the Arizona desert while on the West Coast of the United States, and have spent time in upstate New York, the Berkshires and New Hampshire while on the East Coast. Living in the middle of Europe we are no strangers to the great castles, churches, country houses and museums of many countries. In our own beautiful Australia we really know only the capital cities and beauty spots that are nearby. Next year we will hopefully visit Warsaw for a concert about which we are very excited as it will be our first trip behind the Iron Curtain.

There is still much of the world to see — Joan longs for a Nile cruise and we would both love to see Leningrad, and also Greece and Turkey, so we must retire soon in order to fit in all our trips!

We have received much pleasure in our lives from our public — their more than warm demonstration in the theatre, their lovely letters and, even though sometimes a little tiring after a performance, the long queues waiting for autographs. We have always had great sympathy for the autograph seekers because it doesn't really seem so long ago to us that we were waiting in line for Tauber's autograph or Ninon Vallin's or Georges Thill's.

Many young singers ask Joan how they should have a career like hers. There is no answer to that as in fact we are not even sure why one singer has a major career and another succeeds not at all. Of course, phenomenal vocal cords help and in fact there are few great careers without them. On the other hand, hard work, much luck, physical and mental strength are needed and, above all, individuality. But granted all this we don't really know how it all happened. We are both supremely ordinary people with the most ordinary tastes in the world. We are both full of energy and don't know the meaning of boredom. We love life and are happy it has worked out the way it has. Do have a smile at these pictures which have brought back to us so many happy, amusing and nostalgic memories. But don't ask us how we did it all because we haven't a clue.

Richard Bonynge
May, 1986

ALBUM

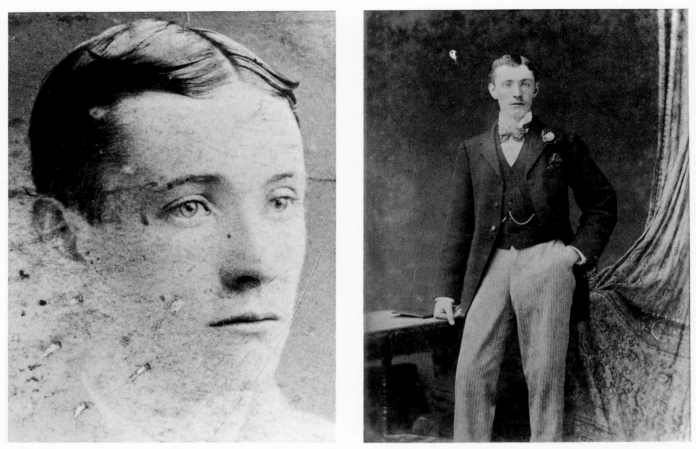

Left: My father about 1890. Taken in Caithness, his home at the northern tip of Scotland. **Right:** Just prior to 1900

Left: My father, *circa* 1910 **Right:** At a Highland gathering in Sydney, 1930, two years before his death (he is standing on the left)

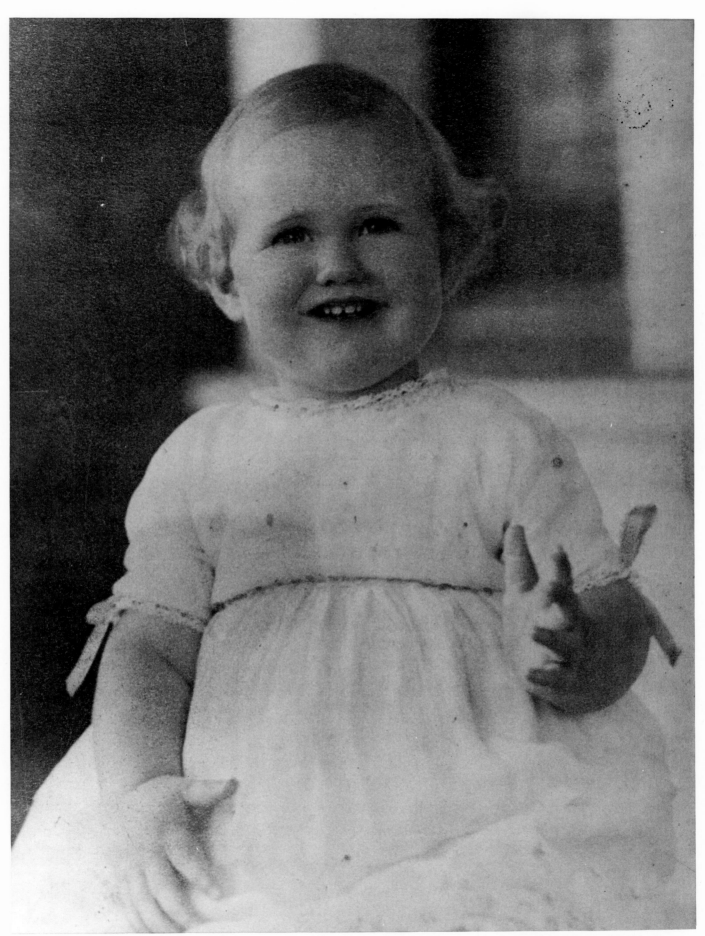

One of the few existing photos of me as a child, about two years old. My dear mother, before she came to London to live with us, decided to get rid of 'all that old rubbish' and burnt a trunkful of old photos. My husband, on the other hand, is an inveterate hoarder

My mother-in-law, Beryl Florence Roughley, *circa*
1927, just before her marriage

Richard's parents' wedding in Sydney 1928

Richard (left) aged about three and (right) about four

With his cousins in the Blue Mountains *circa* 1939 and (right) aged twelve in his Sydney High School uniform

The home of my mother and grandparents, 115 Queen Street, Woollahra, Sydney, and my home from 1932 until 1951 — a watercolour by John van Vliet

A portrait taken in Sydney, *circa* 1949

SOUTH HURSTVILLE METHODIST CHOIR
(Under the Direction of KENNETH STENTON)
Presents

A FAREWELL CONCERT
to
Richard Bonynge, Pianist
(Who is shortly leaving for further study abroad)

METHODIST HALL, ROCKDALE
SATURDAY, JUNE 17, 1950, at 8 p.m.

Richard Bonynge in 1949 won the Open Championship and "Women's Weekly" Scholarship at the Sydney Eisteddfod. A remarkable achievement.

In 1948 he gained the Savage Club Scholarship, Licentiate in Music, and Diplomas for Performer and Teacher. Also the A.M.E.B. Scholarship for the best young pianist in the Commonwealth.

Dr. EDGAR BAINTON said of him: "Richard Bonynge has outstanding ability . . . he is assured of a remarkable career overseas."

ASSOCIATE ARTISTS:
JOAN SUTHERLAND
Winner of "Sun" Aria Contest and a Finalist in the Mobil Quest, 1949.
ALAN FERRIS
Winner of Aria Contest, Melbourne, and a Finalist in the Mobil Quest, 1949.
JUDITH THOMAS (Violiniste).   MARGARET SHERLOCK (Elocutioniste)
Proceeds will be equally divided between Richard Bonynge and the Crippled Children's Fund of the Rotary Club, Hurstville, toward the establishment of the St. George Spastic School.

TICKETS: 3/- and 2/- (May be Obtained at Swans Ltd., Hurstville).
Reservations at Spindler's, Rockdale, and E. G. Hall, Chemist, Bexley.
G. ROSS THOMAS, Chairman of Richard Bonynge Committee.
E. G. HALL, Chairman, St. George Spastic School Committee.

Richard says this must be the only time he got bigger billing than I, when I sang for his going away concert in 1950

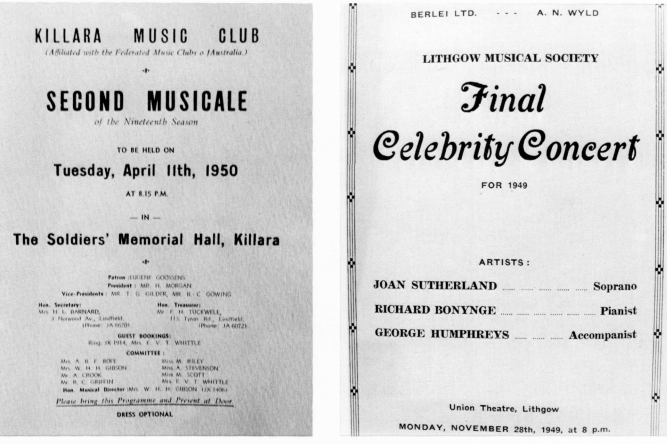

KILLARA   MUSIC   CLUB
(Affiliated with the Federated Music Clubs of Australia.)

SECOND MUSICALE
of the Nineteenth Season

TO BE HELD ON

Tuesday, April 11th, 1950

AT 8.15 P.M.

— IN —

The Soldiers' Memorial Hall, Killara

Patron : EUGENE GOOSSENS
President : MR. H. MORGAN
Vice-Presidents : MR. T. G. GILDER, MR. R. C. GOWING

Hon. Secretary :   Hon. Treasurer :
Mrs. H. L. BARNARD,   Mr. F. H. TUCKWELL,
3 Norwood Av., Lindfield.   113 Tryon Rd., Lindfield.
(Phone: JA 8670)   (Phone: JA 6072)

GUEST BOOKINGS:
Ring JX 1914, Mrs. E. V. T. WHITTLE

COMMITTEE :
Mrs. A. B. F. ROFE   Miss M. RILEY
Mrs. W. H. H. GIBSON   Miss A. STEVENSON
Mr. A. CROOK   Miss M. SCOTT
Mr. R. C. GRIFFIN   Mrs. E. V. T. WHITTLE
Hon. Musical Director (Mrs. W. H. H. GIBSON (JX 1406)

Please bring this Programme and Present at Door.

DRESS OPTIONAL

BERLEI LTD. - - - A. N. WYLD

LITHGOW MUSICAL SOCIETY

Final
Celebrity Concert

FOR 1949

ARTISTS :

JOAN SUTHERLAND .... Soprano

RICHARD BONYNGE .... Pianist

GEORGE HUMPHREYS .... Accompanist

Union Theatre, Lithgow

MONDAY, NOVEMBER 28th, 1949, at 8 p.m.

Early programme announcements

This marks my first staged operatic appearance:
9 June 1951. The composer coached me in the rôle

This is the only pictorial record I have of my operatic stage début, as Judith in Eugene Goossens' opera of that name at the Conservatorium in Sydney, 1951, conducted by the composer. Lina Belle is Haggith. Goossens encouraged me very much and chose me for his opera although I was never a student at the Conservatorium

Left: This was taken shortly after my arrival in London in 1951 **Right:** I sang Amelia in *Un Ballo in Maschera* on 29 December 1952 at Covent Garden. The performance was to have been sung by Elfriede Wasserthal. Both she and Helene Werth were ill and no one else was available. I was third or fourth understudy and was asked to sing the rôle at twelve hours' notice. I somehow survived the ordeal

My student graduation, at the Royal College of Music in 1952. I studied here for one year. I played Giorgetta alongside Gordon Farrell (Michele) in *Il Tabarro*. For years Farrell was a stalwart in the Covent Garden chorus

With fellow student Doreen Langhorn at the Royal College of Music in London, 1952, in an end-of-term scene from *Cosi fan Tutte* when I sang Fiordiligi

Norma, Covent Garden, 1952. My first Bellini rôle, as Clótilde. I felt honoured to be part of these great performances, with Maria Callas in her absolute prime and Ebe Stignani singing wonderfully at an age when most singers have retired

Left: I sang this small but important rôle of Frasquita many times with three different Carmens: Constance Shacklock, Nell Rankin, and Marianna Radev. **Right:** As the Countess in *The Marriage of Figaro* for the first time, in 1953 at Covent Garden. I loved this stately gown of midnight blue velvet designed by Oliver Messel

Covent Garden, 1953, as Helmwige with some of the Valkyries amusing ourselves during a long evening. At the back L — R are Constance Shacklock, Barbara Howitt, and Jean Watson with Monica Sinclair in front. Edith Coates, who is not in the picture, kept the little group very merry with her wicked asides, and Constance had a tendency to trip everyone with her spear

Left: Singing the prayer in Act II of Weber's *Der Freischutz*. I was the second-cast Agathe in this new production at Covent Garden in 1953. **Right:** My mother, Muriel Beatrice Alston Sutherland, taken in Sydney in 1954. She joined us in London and before doing so made a bonfire of all the family photos which accounts for the few existing of my childhood or of my mother, who loathed being photographed. Richard, on the other hand, saves everything!

A rehearsal for the new production of *Das Rheingold* at Covent Garden, *circa* 1954. The Rhinemaidens were hidden in a rock downstage behind a gauze, while dancers mimed the rôles. This was in marked contrast to the former Covent Garden production where we were clad in tights (and I was never the figure for tights) inadequately dotted about with strategically placed pieces of seaweed. I sang Woglinde with Una Hale as Wellgunde, and Marjorie Thomas as Flosshilde. Fritz Stiedry conducted the earlier performances and Rudolf Kempe, the new production

Wearing the John Piper costume for Penelope Rich
in Benjamin Britten's *Gloriana* at Covent Garden
in 1953. This was my *unfavourite* rôle

Left: My first appearance as Antonia in *The Tales of Hoffmann* at the Royal Opera House, 1954. The
production was directed by Gunther Rennert. **Right:** My first Olympia in *The Tales of Hoffmann* at
Covent Garden in 1955. This rôle launched me in the coloratura repertoire. The production was designed
by Georges Wahkevitch

I created the rôle of Jennifer in Michael Tippett's *A Midsummer Marriage* in 1955 at Covent Garden. The vocal line was extremely difficult, and I never understood the story

The world premiere of Michael Tippett's *A Midsummer Marriage*; Act III. With me are Edith Coates as the She-Ancient, Richard Lewis as Mark, and Michael Langdon as the He-Ancient. I found the rôle of Jennifer very challenging and enjoyed it. Edith Coates did not enjoy it and showed her feelings by chewing gum all through the opera. It was known to the cast as 'A Midsummer Miscarriage'

I sang Micaela at Covent Garden in 1955–57 with
Regina Resnik as Carmen

WIGMORE HALL

FRIDAY

OCTOBER 7th, 1955

at 7.30 p.m.

———

INGPEN & WILLIAMS

present

by kind permission of The Royal Opera House, Covent Garden

JOAN SUTHERLAND
(soprano)

Pianoforte: **RICHARD BONYNGE**

The poster for our first recital in London, 1955

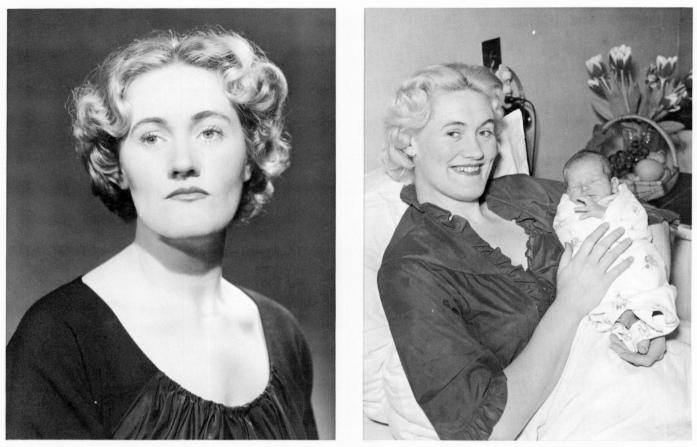

Left: I became a blonde for a short time when I sang Micaela. **Right:** In Queen Charlotte's Hospital, London, following the birth of our son Adam, 13 February 1956

My mother with Adam in the same year

I sang the Countess in *Figaro* for the bicentenary celebrations of the birth of Mozart, at Glyndebourne in 1956. The production was by Carl Ebert with exquisite sets and costumes by Oliver Messel. Michel Roux is seen here as the Count

My début at Covent Garden was as the First Lady in *The Magic Flute* in 1952. This picture was taken at Glyndebourne in 1956 where I sang the same rôle with Cora Canne-Meijer as second, and Monica Sinclair as third ladies

The English painter Roy Hobdell adored *Alcina*
and in 1957 painted this picture of me in the rôle,
complete with magic urn

My first *Alcina*, in the Handel Opera Society production at St Pancras Town Hall in March 1957, directed
by Anthony Besch. The costume was hired; I wore chandelier drops for earrings and was paid the princely
sum of ten pounds for two performances. The opera, which had not been heard in London since the 18th
century, was a musical revelation. Monica Sinclair as Bradamante is on the left, together with the Jamaican
John Carvalho — whom the conductor Charles Farncombe insisted on calling a soprano and not a counter-
tenor. He sounded like the very late records of Clara Butt

Eva in *Die Meistersinger* at Covent Garden in 1957, conducted by Rafael Kubelik and designed by Georges Wahkevitch. Peter Pears sang David in these performances and Geraint Evans, Beckmesser; Hans Sachs was James Pease, and Erich Witte sang Walther

Left: With my mother during the Glyndebourne season in 1957. **Right:** The rôle of Mme Herz in Mozart's *Der Schauspieldirektor* at Glyndebourne in 1957. Rita Streich was to have sung Mme Silberklang with the high F's in alt. She fell ill and Naida Labay took over, leaving me to sing all the high F's — which made me very nervous

As Gilda, Act I, in *Rigoletto*, Covent Garden, 1957.
I did not sing Gilda again until 1972 at the
Metropolitan Opera with Luciano Pavarotti as the
Duke, and both Sherill Milnes and Matteo
Manuguerra as Rigoletto

With Richard Verreau (left) and Otakar Kraus (right) in the same performance of *Rigoletto*, at Covent
Garden. I sang in many operas with Kraus, who was a fine actor and later became a splendid teacher
in London

I created the part of Mme Lidoine in the English première of Poulenc's *Dialogues of the Carmelites* at Covent Garden in January 1958. When shown my photos in the rôle, the Mother Superior of a Carmelite convent said I had the face of a true daughter of Carmel.

Left: The opera was conducted by Rafael Kubelik and directed by Margherita Wallmann. Poulenc supervised all rehearsals. **Right:** The New Prioress in the last act, just before going to the guillotine

Upper: As Donna Anna in *Don Giovanni* at the Vancouver Festival, 1958. This was my first engagement on the American continent. **Middle:** An informal shot taken during the Vancouver Festival. *Don Giovanni* was directed by Gunther Rennert on the right, next to George London (Giovanni) and designed by Ita Maximovna (top right). George was impressed and arranged an audition at the Metropolitan Opera immediately following the Festival. I sang Caro Nome and failed the audition. This was only a few months before my first *Lucia*. **Lower:** Leopold Simoneau sang Don Ottavio to my Donna Anna

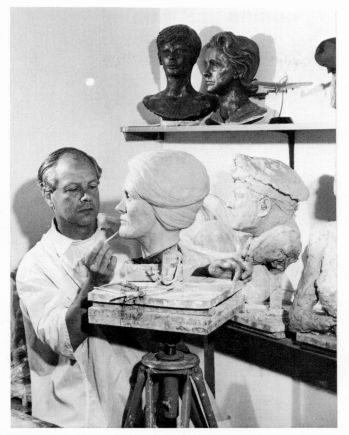

Being sculpted in about 1958 by my former dentist Henry Pitt-Roche. I loathe being sculpted, as I always end up looking like Beethoven.

With Her Majesty the Queen and Prince Philip after the Royal Command Performance of Handel's *Samson* in 1958

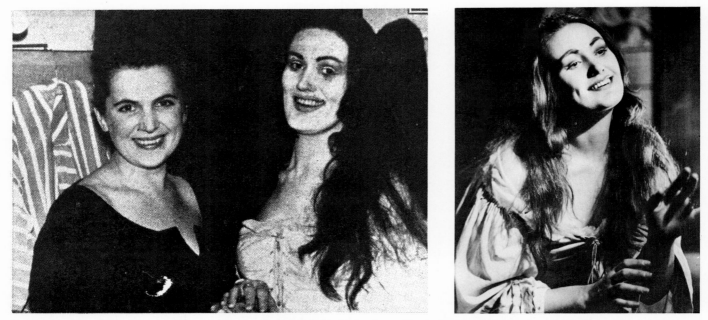

Left: Galina Vishnevskaya visited me on the last night of my first series of Lucias on 28 February, 1959. We in turn went to see her as Aida, a performance always interesting and motivated by real theatrical intelligence. We met again many years later at the opera in San Francisco when she was performing in *The Queen of Spades* with her husband Mstislav Rostropovich conducting. **Right:** The 'Mad Scene' in my first performance of *Lucia*. Covent Garden, 17 February 1959. The production, sets, and costumes were all by Franco Zeffirelli, who found the way to give me real dramatic confidence. This was the first time I sang with Tullio Serafin, who gave me a sixpence the first time he heard my high E♭. The cast included Kenneth Neate, Edgardo; Geraint Evans, Enrico; Michael Langdon, Raimondo; and Kenneth MacDonald, Arturo

At home. London, 1959

The cover of *Theatre World* in April 1959 after my
success as Lucia. I was the second Australian
soprano to sing *Lucia* at Covent Garden; the first
was Melba

I don't remember what wisecrack prompted this expression when Maria Callas visited me backstage in
1959. Maria was always very friendly and sent notes and flowers to my opening nights. We appeared
together in The Covent Garden Centenary Gala in June 1958. We had performed together in *Norma* (when
I sang Clotilde) in 1952 and in *Aida* (I was the high priestess) in 1953, but these were the only times.
Callas was originally announced to sing Valentine when I sang Queen Marguerite at La Scala in 1962,
but for some reason or other changed her mind. Giulietta Simionato sang the rôle in her place

Lucia at Covent Garden, 1959. Zeffirelli and Serafin had quite a row over the blood stains on Lucia's costume. Serafin thought it was in bad taste but Zeffirelli argued that a woman who had stabbed her husband numerous times could hardly appear in pristine white. The blood has remained

Left: The cover of *Opera* magazine after my first Covent Garden Lucia. **Right:** The title rôle in Handel's *Rodelinda* for the Handel Opera Society at Sadler's Wells in 1959

Left: Donna Anna, at the Vienna State Opera in 1959. The Viennese press kindly said I was the greatest Donna Anna since their own Lilli Lehmann **Right:** Richard with Maestro Tullio Serafin in Venice, 1959

Richard snapped me unawares picking heather in Scotland in 1959

With Adam in Cornwall Gardens, London, the same year

Left: I try a new look

Below: When I sang my first Violetta in 1960 at Covent Garden, the production was an old one designed in the late 1940s by Sophie Fedorowitch. Franco Zeffirelli designed four costumes for me. This is the Act III dress of ruby red velvet with a necklace of jet

La Traviata, Covent Garden, 1960. I did not actually wear this costume on stage — it was an early publicity shot

From the same performance of *La Traviata* with Marie Collier as Flora and John Dobson as Gaston

With Sir David Webster in the Crush Bar at Covent Garden, *circa* 1960

The Glyndebourne production of *Don Giovanni*, 1960. The director was Carl Ebert and the designer, Ita Maximovna. L — R: Mirella Freni as Zerlina, Ilva Ligabue as Donna Elvira, Geraint Evans as Leporello, and Ernest Blanc as Don Giovanni

Two 1960 cover designs: *Records Magazine* (February Issue) and *The Art of the Prima Donna* — the latter designed by Roy Hobdell

Dressing Room, Palermo, 1960 — a performance of
Lucia

The Théatres Lyriques Nationaux programme for a Paris *Lucia* in 1960

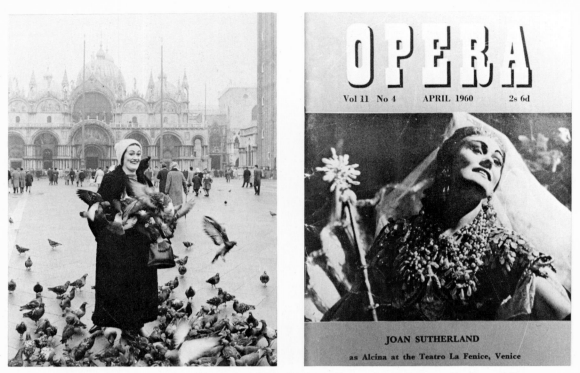

Left: Just another tourist in Venice, 1960. In fact, I was here for my Italian début.
Right: Cover of *Opera*, April 1960

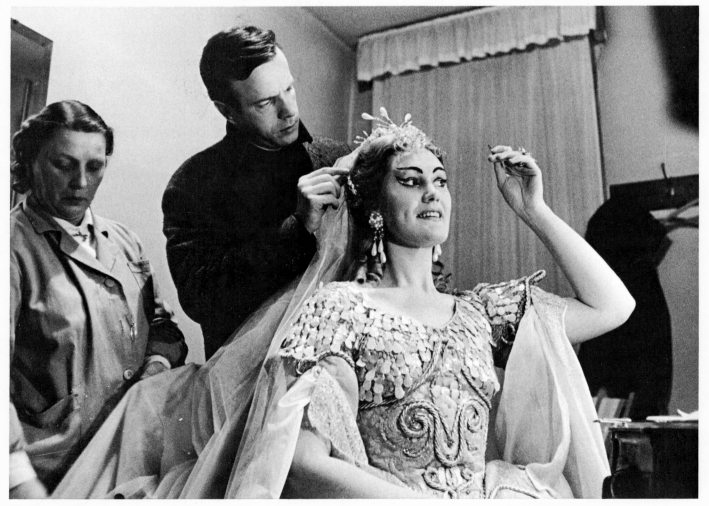

Franco Zeffirelli not only designed the sets of *Alcina* (Teatro Fenice: 1960) but supervised their making and that of the costumes by Anna Anni, down to the smallest details. Indeed, this lavishly beautiful production showed the results of his meticulous care. After Venice it went on to Dallas where Blanche Thebom sang the part of Ruggiero and where I made my American operatic début on 16 November 1960

"BETTER THAN CALLAS"

FROM JEAN HOGAN IN LONDON

"LA STUPENDA," as the Italians call John Sutherland, has now, in the view of a Milan newspaper (not a safe place to air such views unless they happen to be generally regarded as true), "surpassed Callas as the world's

There is only one absolute and shining confirmation that you are a prima donna of international importance—and it arrived by post a few weeks ago for Miss Joan Sutherland.

It was a letter asking her to sing at La Scala, Milan, for two months, April

Left: *Alcina*, at the Teatro Fenice in Venice, 1960. **Right:** The 'Mad Scene' from *Lucia*, Palermo, 1960. Conducted by Serafin and directed by Zeffirelli. These performances included Gianni Raimondi as Edgardo and Mario Zanasi as Enrico

Franco Zeffirelli puts a finishing touch to the Act II costume in *Lucia*; Palermo, 1960

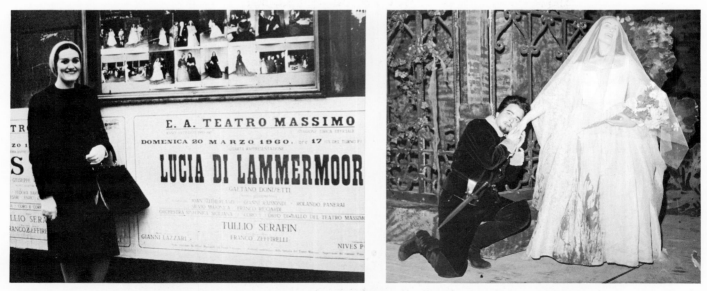

Left: In Palermo at the time of my first Italian *Lucia* **Right:** With Alain Vanzo in the Tomb Scene of *Lucia* at the Opéra in Paris, 1960. These were the only performances where Lucia rose from the grave à la Giselle

Left: With Maurice Chevalier at Maxim's in Paris, 1960 **Right:** This dressing room, hung with rose silk at the Opéra in Paris, was the personal property of the great French soprano, Fanny Heldy, who as a special courtesy let me use it

As Desdemona in Verdi's *Otello* at the Staatsoper in Vienna, 1959. My Otello on this occasion was Carlos Guichandut. I previously sang the rôle at Covent Garden with Ramon Vinay as Otello in 1957

This was my first *I Puritani*. Arturo was Nicola
Filacuridi; Riccardo, Ernest Blanc; and Giorgio,
Giuseppe Modesti; Glyndebourne, 1960. Vittorio
Gui conducted, Gianfranco Enriquez directed, and
Desmond Heeley designed. I sang in the same
production at the Edinburgh Festival later that
year

During the production of *I Puritani*, we stayed at the
old manor of Johnstonburn outside Edinburgh

Rehearsing with Francesco Molinari-Pradelli in the Kingsway Hall, London, for *The Art of the Prima Donna*, one of the best-selling operatic sets ever made. This was in 1960, and he conducted my San Francisco début as Lucia in the following year

Amina, a role I love dearly, at Covent Garden in 1960. The theatre gave me a new production by Enrico Medioli with sets and costumes by Filippo Sanjust

I Puritani at the Teatro Liceo, Barcelona, 1960.
The great Spanish baritone Manuel Ausensi sang
Riccardo, and Gianni Iaia, Arturo

Serafin rehearsing me in *La Sonnambula* at Covent Garden, 1960

Franco Zeffirelli took this photo of me as Donna
Anna in his production in Dallas, 1960, which he
designed and directed. Elisabeth Schwarzkopf
sang Donna Elvira; Eugenia Ratti, Zerlina; Liugi
Alva, Ottavio; Eberhard Waechter, the Don; and
Giuseppe Taddei, Leporello

Left: *I Puritani* at the Teatro Massimo, Palermo, 1961, with (L — R) Mario Zanasi (Riccardo), Vera
Magrini (the Queen), Peter John Hall who designed the costumes, and Gianni Raimondi (Arturo).
Zeffirelli directed **Right:** I only appeared once with Sir John Gielgud although we spent a wonderful
holiday together at Franco Zeffirelli's villa in Castiglioncello. In March 1961 we were guests on a
Shakespearean programme in which Sir John read some famous passages and I sang arias of Ophelia
and Desdemona

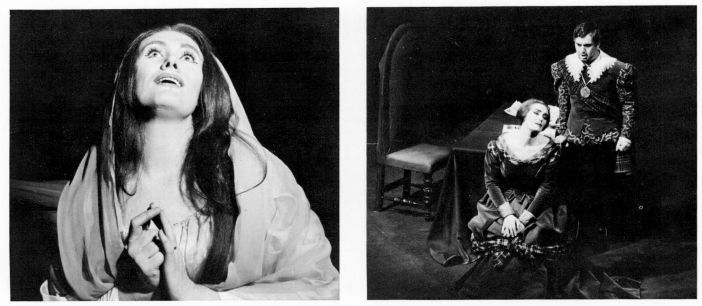

Left: The 'Mad Scene' from *Lucia*, La Scala 1961 **Right:** From the same performance with Ettore Bastianini as Enrico. He also sang the opera with me in Dallas, Texas

Her Majesty Queen Elizabeth and the Duke of Edinburgh visit backstage at La Scala in 1961 for an act of *Lucia di Lammermoor*. On the right, standing next to Nicola Benois, is Gianni Raimondi, who sang Edgardo

Left: Cover of *Vita*, August 1961

ANNO III · VOL. VI · N. 121 · 10 AGOSTO 1961 · LIRE 100

VITA

SETTIMANALE DI N

BERLINO O IL FASCINO DELL'ABISSO

POLIO: VACCINO DI SALK O DI SABIN?

JOAN SUTHERLAND

THE VOICE THAT THRILLED LA SCALA

Australia's Joan Sutherland has reached the goal of every opera singer and been acclaimed as "the greatest" at her debut

Left: As Bellini's tragic Beatrice di Tenda, the second rôle I sang in Milan.
Right: I felt like the wicked Queen in Snow White in this horrible costume, which is also from *Beatrice di Tenda*. Giuseppe Campora sang the tenor rôle of Orombello. We later recorded the opera with Luciano Pavarotti, Josephine Veasey, and Cornelis Opthof. *Beatrice* was the opera chosen for my New York début on 21 February 1961 in the Town Hall. This was the first time Marilyn Horne and I appeared together. Marilyn sang Agnese

Lucia at the Teatro Fenice, Venice, 1961, with Renato Cioni as Edgardo. Cioni brought great passion to this part

The 'Mad Scene' at La Scala, 1961

Left: We grew up with the recordings of Amelita Galli-Curci, and when I received a telegram from her at the time of my San Francisco début we were thrilled. We drove down to Rancho Santa Fe near San Diego to visit her and found the tiniest, sweetest lady covered from top to toe in pink. She gave us one great piece of advice: that we alone must be the judges of what was right for us in our career, to 'put on ze blinders like ze 'orse and look straight ahead'. Advice duly followed to this day . . . **Right:** This funny old picture makes me laugh. My Metropolitan Opera début in *Lucia*, 1961, with Richard Tucker as Edgardo. We also sang *Lucia* in Chicago as well as many performances of *La Traviata* at the Metropolitan

During the Edinburgh Festival in 1961 for *Lucia*, I visited the graveyard at Lammermoor

With Franco Zeffirelli after my Chicago début as
Lucia in 1961

Lucia, Metropolitan Opera, 1961. Jan Peerce as well as his brother-in-law, Richard Tucker, sang with
me in this production. The by-then-decrepit production dated from 1942 in the days of Lily Pons

Left: *I Puritani* in Palermo, 1961 **Right:** With darling Maestro Serafin, in the same production

At one of Geri Souvaine's parties in New York. L — R back row: Regina Resnik, Frederic March, Birgit Nilsson, Giovanni Martinelli. L — R front row: John Brownlee, Robert Merrill, Nicola Moscona

I must have said something to amuse Birgit Nilsson, Alexandra Danilova, and Florence Eldridge.
This is taken at a party given for us by Geri Souvaine after my Metropolitan Opera début in 1961

Richard, *circa* 1962

Alberto Erede conducted concerts for me in Antwerp and Amsterdam in February 1962 (my Belgian and Dutch débuts) and for *La Traviata* at Covent Garden the following month

Mementos from 1962

I sang Amina in Bellini's *La Sonnambula* in the
beautiful Visconti prodution at La Scala designed
by Piero Tosi in 1962. Antonino Votto conducted
and Alfredo Kraus was Elvino

The enchanting balletic production of *La Sonnambula* was the most beautiful we have ever encountered

This photo was taken during the Covent Garden production of *Alcina* in 1962 which had been borrowed from Venice

Beatrice di Tenda at the Teatro San Carlo in Naples, 1962, one of the most beautiful and acoustically perfect theatres in the world. Renata Cioni was splendid as Orombello. I loved singing the tragic Queen Beatrice

Giulietta Simionato was one of the true 'grandes dames' of opera. I sang with her in both *Les Huguenots* (or more precisely, *Gli Ugonotti*) and *Semiramide* at La Scala

Left: With Giulietta Simionato in Act II of *Les Huguenots* at La Scala. Franco Corelli sang Raoul; Fiorenza Cossotto, Urbain; Nicolai Ghiaurov, Marcel; Giorgio Tozzi, St Bris; and Wladimiro Ganzarolli, Nevers. The opera was conducted by Gianandrea Gavazzeni, directed by Gianfranco Enriquez, and designed by Nicola Benois **Right:** The entrance of Queen Marguerite in Act III of *Les Huguenots*. The horse was called George and made some very peculiar comments during the performance. On one occasion my page Fiorenza Cossotto, who was to the rear of the horse, was seen to turn a rather ghastly shade of green

The Queen of the Night at Covent Garden conducted by Otto Klemperer in 1962

Left: After the 'Mad Scene' in *Lucia*, Barcelona 1962. The tiny part of Arturo in this production was sung by Giacomo Aragall. Placido Domingo had sung this rôle with me in Dallas the year before and Guy Chauvet sang it in Paris in 1960. Perhaps it brought them luck!

Below: The lovely old Teatro Liceo in Barcelona, 1962.

On stage after the opening night of *Semiramide* at La Scala, Milan, in December 1962. This photograph shows Giulietta Simionato in her Arsace costume; Margherita Wallmann, the director; Nicola Benois, the designer; and Wladimiro Ganzarolli, Assur

A curtain call after *Semiramide* with Giulietta Simionato and the grand old Maestro Gabriele Santini. He was at the same time one of the most bad-tempered and most lovable of conductors. He broke batons, demolished the conductor's desk, threw his score at the orchestra, and walked out with astonishing regularity. But how he understood Rossinian style!

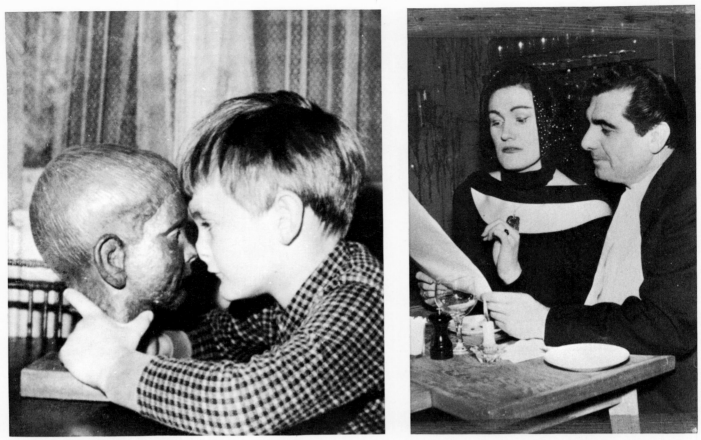

Left: Adam was very taken with this sculpture of himself by Henry Pitt-Roche done in October 1962
Right: Supper with Geraint Evans in London, *circa* 1962

At a party given by Geri Souvaine in New York in 1962. L — R: Silvio Varviso, Regina Resnik, Ania Dorfmann, Bidu Sayäo, Nicola Moscona, Jennie Tourel, Thelma Votipka, and Robert Merrill

HALF-HOUR OF APPLAUSE FOR AUST. SINGER

LONDON, Mon. — For 30 thundering minutes, London's Albert Hall roared acclamation of Australian prima donna Joan Sutherland last night.

One newspaper critic said Miss Sutherland gave the "most stupendous exhibition of sheer singing I have heard."

Four times during the evening her voice floated effortlessly up to the "stratospheric heights" of top E flat.

The critic said her coloratura was "dazzling as the purest sapphires set on a bed of soft velvet."

Miss Sutherland encored the end of the aria.

The audience clamor-

"Retire now? No. I'll go on singing till I drop."

Her husband and coach, Richard Bonynge, added: "All the papers have exaggerated Joan's arthritic trouble."

Miss Sutherland said the pain from her flattened disc had not been troubling her much before the concert.

"It does give me a twinge when I take deep breaths," she said.

"But don't worry. I'll

STATE DINNER
IN HONOR OF
JOAN SUTHERLAND
THE LOTOS CLUB
JANUARY 24, 1963

Left: The Lotos Club in New York City honoured me in 1963. The drawing, commissioned for the occasion, is of Queen Marguerite in *Les Huguenots* in the La Scala costume. I was subsequently made an Honorary Member of the club

I am pulling a face again! With Leonard Bernstein in the Philharmonic Hall on 26 March 1963. The gown was by Arnold Scaasi and the hair-do, Mr Adolfo

I sang with Ella Fitzgerald and Dinah Shore in 1963 on the NBC Dinah Shore Show. Apart from my first act aria from *La Traviata*, we sang together a not-too D'Oyly Carte version of the 'Three Little Maids from School' and 'Lover Come Back to Me'. We went soon after to hear a concert by Ella Fitzgerald — her brilliant improvisation could teach many classical singers a thing or two

Listening to a playback of 'The Age of Bel Canto'
with Marilyn Horne in London, 1963

After yet another first night of *Lucia* in the 1960s, but I can't remember which one

The new production at the Metropolitan Opera of *La Sonnambula*, in February 1963, was directed by Henry Butler and designed by Rolf Gérard, who gave me fitted chiffon costumes which made me look fat. Not so strangely, I can find few photographic records of these as I used them only for a few performances and then wore my beautiful Tosi costume from La Scala which they graciously gave me

The same production of *La Sonnambula*, with Nicolai Gedda as Elvino

Press clippings, 1963

My first *Norma*, Act I, Vancouver, 1963, directed by Irving Guttman and designed by Suzanne Mess. This was the first of many performances which I was to sing with Marilyn Horne as Adalgisa — a happy partnership which continued at Covent Garden, the Metropolitan Opera (and on tour with the Met), in San Francisco, and on recordings

Taken by the East River in New York, *circa* 1963

Left: Geri Souvaine was the directress of the Texaco Opera broadcasts from the Metropolitan Opera. She gave us great encouragement and friendship and some spectacular parties **Right:** With Marilyn Horne after one of our concerts in the United States in the early 1960s

Curtain call after Act I of *La Traviata* with Nicolai
Gedda during the Metropolitan Opera broadcast
performance on 11 January 1964

Taken in the garden of the Villa San Michele in Fiesole where we were
staying while making a recording of *La Sonnambula* in 1963

In the 'Mad Scene' of *I Puritani*, Boston 1964. This was directed by Sarah Caldwell

Two shots from *I Puritani*, Act I, Covent Garden 1964. In the photograph below I am with Joseph Rouleau

As Elvira in the 'Mad Scene' of *I Puritani* at Covent Garden, 1964. A wonderful production by Franco Zeffirelli

I judged the costumes with Carlo Maria Giulini and Sir Frederick Ashton for the 1964 Opera Ball at Grosvenor House in London

Adam spent some time with us in New York in 1964

Right: At a Gala in Philadelphia at the Academy of Music with the Philadelphia Symphony Orchestra. Leopold Stokowski conducted my 'Mad Scene' in *Lucia* and Franco Corelli was my co-star. Stokowski was so enchanted by the cadenza that he forgot to bring in the orchestra at the end and left me high but not dry on the E♭ for quite some time

Angus McBean took many beautiful photographs. London *circa* 1964

A Gala at the Metropolitan on 29 November 1964,
with Renata Tebaldi, Elisabeth Schwarzkopf and
Lisa della Casa. Elisabeth Schwarzkopf and Lisa
della Casa sang in the first act of *Der
Rosenkavalier*, Renata Tebaldi in *La Bohème* Act I,
and I sang in the first act of *La Traviata*

New York, *circa* 1964. This photograph was taken for *Opera News* by the famous Japanese
photographer, Hiro

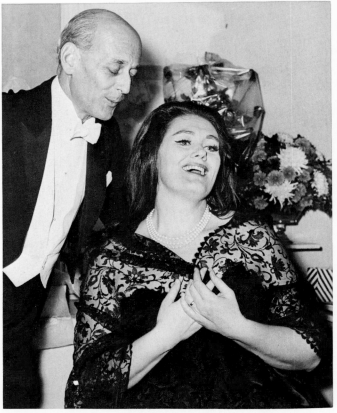

Right: I opened the season at the old Metropolitan Opera House with *Lucia* on 12 November, 1964. Rudolf Bing, then General Manager, offered his congratulations. During Bing's term at the Met, I sang a great deal of my repertoire, all of which Richard conducted after the first few seasons. Bing also gave Richard a new production of Gluck's *Orfeo* as well as *Il Barbiere di Siviglia* with Teresa Berganza

Left: Dame Judith Anderson, the great Australian actress, visited me after my opening night in *Lucia* at the Metropolitan in 1964. We saw her in her great part, Medea, many times, and in 1983 in New York she played the Nurse to Zoe Caldwell's Medea — unforgettable performances **Right:** Recording at Kingsway Hall, London, *circa* 1964

Left: As Violetta at Covent Garden, 1962. **Right:** When Renato Cioni cancelled *Lucia* in Miami in 1965 at the last moment, we suggested the young tenor whom we had engaged for our Australian tour the same year. Thus Luciano Pavarotti made his American début

Lucia, Act I, in Copenhagen with tenor Doro Antonioli, 1966

Noël Coward painted Richard's portrait on holiday
in Jamaica in 1965. Noël did not think it was his
best effort, but it was a lovely souvenir for us

On holiday in Jamaica. Peter Sellers and Britt Ekland in the garden at 'Firefly', Noël Coward's mountain
eyrie, April 1965

In Noël Coward's jeep, with Peter Sellers, Britt Ekland, Noël, Cole Lesley, and Weenie, my secretary

Rehearsing with Noël Coward for our record *Joan Sutherland sings Noël Coward*. This was also taken at 'Firefly' in April 1965

Left: Singing 'Bel Raggio Lusinghier' in *Semiramide*, during the 1965 Australian tour. Norman Ayrton directed the opera and Tonina Dorati designed. Monica Sinclair sang Arsace and was wont to improvise her cadenzas. On a good day she would hurtle from a middle C to the C two octaves higher and then plunge three octaves to the C in the bass stave. I am not exaggerating! **Right:** A performance of *La Traviata* during the 1965 Australian tour. The photograph shows Joseph Ward (Gaston) and Luciano Pavarotti (Alfredo), with Monica Sinclair hiding behind her fan. Next to her is the Australian bass Donald Shanks, who was then in the chorus

From the Sutherland-Williamson Grand Opera Season in 1965. In this Melbourne performance of *La Sonnambula*, Dorothy Cole is Teresa and Luciano Pavarotti, Elvino

Ruthli came to us as Adam's nanny when he was one year old in 1957. She is still with us, is one of our family, and looks after us as if we were Royalty. Here we are visiting the zoo at Taronga Park, Sydney, 1965

Left: For several seasons our tours and those of Marcel Marceau coincided all over the world. Here we are backstage in Sydney in 1965, but it might as well have been Hamburg, Vancouver, or London **Right:** I went to the theatre to hear *Lucia di Lammermoor* at one of the few performances when I was not singing the rôle myself during our 1965 Australian tour. Luciano Pavarotti was singing with Elizabeth Harwood, the English soprano.

The Melbourne season of the Sutherland-Williamson Opera Company in 1965 closed with *La Sonnambula* and was one of the most memorable and emotional evenings in our lives, a true welcome home to our country. The whole company came on stage and the audience stayed in the theatre and refused to go until an old piano was wheeled in and I sang 'Home Sweet Home'. The cast included Luciano Pavarotti, Elizabeth Harwood, Lauris Elms, and Spiro Malas

Another photograph of the last night of *La Sonnambula*

Left: The *Australian Women's Weekly*, July cover of 1965 with John Alexander in *Lucia* **Right:** I sang Marguerite in *Faust* on our Australian tour in 1965, my first return since I left in 1951. This was perhaps the last grand old-fashioned opera tour — the Company gave eight performances a week for fourteen weeks in Melbourne, Adelaide, Sydney, and Brisbane

Left: After the opening night in Melbourne of our 1965 tour, with Sir Frank and Lady Tait. Sir Frank was the last of the four Tait brothers who managed the theatrical firm J. C. Williamson's, which had been founded by the American actor of that name who settled in Australia in the 1860s. Sir Frank had been involved with presenting the Melba-Williamson opera seasons in his youth and wanted to end his career with a Sutherland-Williamson season. He died just after the first five weeks of the season, having witnessed some of the greatest ovations in Australian theatre **Right:** Tony Rafty did this cartoon of me in Sydney in 1965. I'm obviously a cartoonist's delight!

Left: Taken in my dressing room in Adelaide, August 1965 **Right:** Richard on the beach during the 1965 Australian tour with Elizabeth Harwood and Morag Beaton (front), Margreta Elkins, Spiro Malas, Martin Scheepers, and Joy Mammen — all members of the Company

Rigby drew this cartoon in 1965 after we were so audacious as to give our opinion of the press. It's a favourite

Noël Coward gives Adam a painting lesson in his
studio in 1965

Portrait of Richard, Toronto *circa* 1965

Left: The Lesson Scene in *The Daughter of the Regiment* with Monica Sinclair as the Marquise, Covent Garden 1966 **Right:** As the regimental drummer in the same opera

With Her Majesty, Queen Elizabeth the Queen Mother, just after a Gala performance of *The Daughter of the Regiment*. Directly behind me are Monica Sinclair and Edith Coates

Left: Pavarotti as Tonio and Spiro Malas as Sergeant Sulpice in the Act II trio, *The Daughter of the Regiment,* Covent Garden, 1966 **Right:** Act I of *The Daughter* at Covent Garden with Pavarotti and Malas. This charming production was done by Sandro Sequi with sets by Anna Anni and costumes by Marcel Escoffier

Left: The crack-shot at Covent Garden in 1966. I never liked the pants that Marcel Escoffier designed for *The Daughter of the Regiment* and after the first production asked Barbara Matera to make me a new costume after the style of Jenny Lind's **Right:** Dancing lesson for Act II of *The Daughter of the Regiment* Alan Vautrain is the ballet master

Left: The cover of the Noël Coward record, 1966 **Middle:** This photo was made when I was recording Noël's songs and it was used on the back of the album. I think he rather enjoyed coaching me in how to sing his songs **Right:** Ladybird Johnson came to a performance of *I Puritani* in San Francisco in 1966

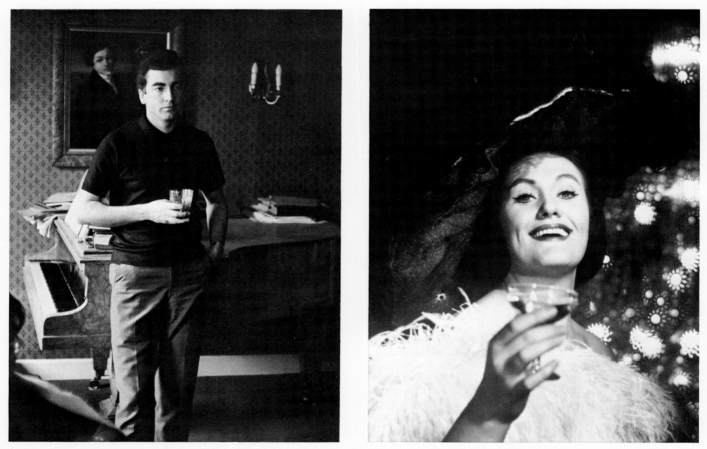

Left: In our London studio, 1966. The picture behind Richard is of the Count Belgiojoso, a pupil of Rossini **Right:** Taken in the Crush Bar at Covent Garden, *circa* 1966. A similar picture was used on the cover of our two-record album *Love Live Forever* (in America: *The Golden Age of Operetta*) recorded in 1966

Left: Alfredo Kraus was a perfect partner in *I Puritani* in San Francisco in 1966 **Right:** *Norma* at Covent Garden with Franco Tagliavini, 1967. I loved singing with this fine tenor, who towered over me

This portrait was painted in London by June Mendoza in 1967, and now hangs in our Swiss home

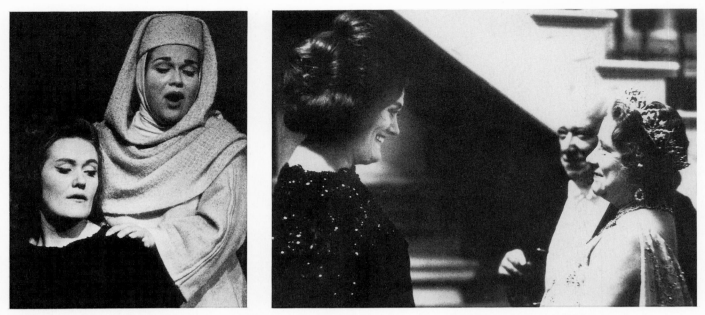

Left: Covent Garden mounted a new production of *Norma* for me in 1967, with Marilyn Horne as Adalgisa. The production was directed by Sandro Sequi and designed by Pier Luigi Pizzi **Right:** With Her Majesty Queen Elizabeth the Queen Mother and Sir David Webster after a Gala at Covent Garden in 1967. The programme included Act IV of *Don Carlos* with Grace Bumbry and Boris Christoff and the 'Mad Scene' from *Lucia di Lammermoor*

Our chalet in the Alps above Montreux, Switzerland

Euridice in Haydn's *Orfeo ed Euridice* at the
Theater an den Wien in 1967. Although this opera
was written in 1801, it was never produced in
Haydn's day. We gave the first Viennese
performances of this work over a century and a half
later, and also at the Edinburgh Festival. The
production was by Rudolf Hartmann

Again, as Euridice with Nicolai Gedda as Orfeo, at the Theater an der Wien. This lovely Viennese theatre
saw the première of *Fidelio* and *Die Fledermaus*

In my Act III costume as Lakmé in the Seattle
production, 1967

My costume for *Lakmé* was made of green crystal cabochons, it weighed a ton and gouged deep furrows
in my shoulders. Many were appalled that I would wear green on the stage, not to mention peacock
feathers, both of which are considered unlucky in some quarters

I sang with Tito Gobbi in a scene from *Rigoletto* and one from the second act of *Tosca* on the Bell Telephone Hour for American television in 1968. Gobbi tried to persuade me to sing *Tosca* on the stage with him in Europe. I didn't feel it was right at the time but regret that I did not work further with this consummate artist

Left: A *Norma* curtain call in Philadelphia, 1968, with Bernabé Marti as Pollione. Montserrat Caballé came to this performance to hear her husband sing with me **Right:** With Sandro Sequi backstage at the Maggio Musicale in Florence, 1968, during a rehearsal of Rossini's *Semiramide*. Verdi does not seem to approve. The production was directed by Sequi and designed by Pier Luigi Samaritani, with costumes by Peter J. Hall

Left: I sang many performances for the Bell Telephone Hour on American television. This one on 22 March 1968 was called 'Two to Six' and consisted of operatic ensembles from duet up to sextet. In the back row are Charles Anthony, Nicolai Gedda, Jerome Hines, Tito Gobbi, and Phyllis Curtin. Mildred Miller, the mezzo-soprano, is seated **Right:** We did a semi-staged performance of *Les Huguenots* in the Royal Albert Hall, London, in 1968. Martina Arroyo sang Valentine; Huguette Tourangeau, Urbain; Anastasios Vrenios, Raoul; Nicola Ghiuselev, Marcel; Robert El Hage, St Bris; and Dominic Cossa, Nevers. Most of these singers sang on the complete recording made soon after

Photographed at a New York party in 1968 with fabled film star Dolores del Rio

Donna Anna with Gabriel Bacquier as Don Giovanni in Seattle, April 1968. This great artist later sang Leporello with me at the Metropolitan Opera

Left: Decca made this stunning cover for our recording of *La Fille du Regiment* in 1968 **Right:** The French arias were recorded in 1969

As Cleopatra in the Hamburg production of Handel's *Giulio Cesare*, 1969. I had previously sung this rôle in London for the Handel Opera Society, in 1963

Left: As Cleopatra in Tito Capobianco's superb production of *Giulio Cesare* at the Hamburg Opera in 1969. The gorgeous costumes were by José Varona, and sets by Ming Cho Lee **Right:** Huguette Tourangeau played Caesar to my Cleopatra. We performed this opera fifteen times in Hamburg during 1969 and 1971, Lucia Popp and Tom Krause both sang in the production

Left: *La Traviata*, Act I, Teatro Colon, Buenos Aires, 1969. Sandro Sequi directed, Renato Cioni was Alfredo, and Piero Cappuccilli, Germont **Right:** *Norma* in the same theatre, directed by Sandro Sequi and designed by Pier Luigi Pizzi. The Teatro Colon has possibly the greatest acoustics of all the big theatres. Fiorenza Cossotto sang Adalgisa and Charles Craig, Pollione

At the Gala Tribute Performance of *Falstaff* for Sir David Webster in April 1980. L — R: Regina Resnik and Geraint Evans, Amy Shuard on my left, and then the Earl of Drogheda. Sir David Webster is supporting a large laurel wreath with Joseph Rouleau and Gwyneth Jones on his right. On his left are Delme Bryn-Jones, Edgar Evans, and Ryland Davies

Left: At a party in London with Dame Alicia Markova and Dame Eva Turner — it would be hard to find two more energetic, charming and interesting Dames than these. Unfortunately we never heard Dame Eva sing, but we cut our ballet teeth with Dame Alicia. She taught Richard all the correct tempi for his first ballet set 'The Art of the Prima Ballerina'. She would sing the tunes and make her fingers dance the steps on the table **Right:** Ania Dorfmann was a very great pianist and a very dear friend. She was a favourite pianist of Toscanini who made several extraordinary recordings with her, notably the Mendelssohn G Minor and Beethoven G Major concertos. When Richard began conducting in 1962, she came to innumerable rehearsals, encouraging and helping with sound advice. She continued to do so until her death in 1984

Signing autographs in San Francisco, *circa* 1970

Left: *Norma* curtain call at the Metropolitan Opera in 1970 with Carlo Bergonzi, Marilyn Horne, and Cesare Siepi **Right:** Desmond Heeley's stunning gold costume for *Norma*. The production was directed by Paul-Emile Deiber

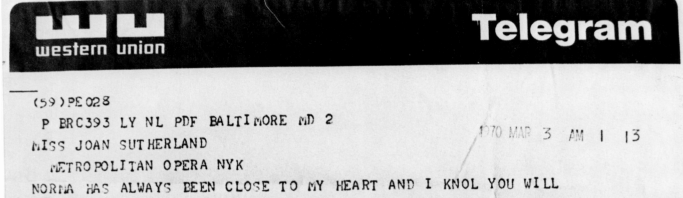

I felt honoured and encouraged to receive this telegram from Rosa Ponselle, a very great Norma

Left: José Varona did this drawing for Richard's fortieth birthday. We use it for our bookplate and some stationery **Right:** James Mason, 1970. He and his wife Clarissa Kay lived close to us in Switzerland

With President and Mrs Richard Nixon, John Browning, and Placido Domingo after a concert at the Academy of Music, Philadelphia, 1970. The concert celebrated one hundred and thirteen years of the Academy, seventy years of the Philadelphia Orchestra, and Eugene Ormandy's seventieth birthday. He conducted the concert and I sang the Queen's aria from *Les Huguenots* and the *Lucia* duet with Domingo

Left: The 'Mad Scene', *Lucia di Lammermoor* Hamburg, 1971 **Right:** The same scene, with Kurt Moll as Raimondo in the background

With Placido Domingo as Edgardo in the Hamburg production of *Lucia*, 1971. In this sensitive and dramatic production by Peter Beauvais we played the opera uncut. Domingo and Tom Krause had enormous success in the Wolfcrag Scene

With Tom Krause who played Enrico. Some very old people were hired from a home for retired circus and theatrical performers and they were rivetting in the Wedding Scene

With Placido Domingo in Hamburg

Maria Stuarda, San Francisco, 1971. The photograph was printed on canvas and brushstroked, and gives the illusion of a painting

Left: The cover of our 1971 recording of *Lucia* has a portrait painted by June Mendoza **Right** On the balcony of the Chalet Coward in Les Avants. L — R: Graham Payn, Wendy Toye, Cole Lesley, Sir Noël Coward and Lady Diana Cooper, *circa* 1971

Richard with Sir Noël in the Chalet Coward at Les Avants, Christmas 1971

Left: A record shop window display in Hamburg **Right:** In Les Avants with English actor Robert Stevens, 1971

In the television studios at Shepperton, 1972. *The Barber of Seville* was produced by Ted Kotcheff, whose language was ripe and direction inspiring. Made with the intention of introducing children to opera, the series captured a wide adult public. We played *Lucia di Lammermoor*, *The Daughter of the Regiment*, *Faust*, *La Traviata*, *Rigoletto*, *La Perichole* and *Mignon*. Most of the series is now available on MGM video cassettes

Left: Rosina in *The Barber of Seville* with Spiro Malas as Dr Bartolo, and Ramon Remedios as Count Almaviva for our 1972 television series *Who's Afraid of Opera?* **Right:** Philine in Thomas' *Mignon*, which was included in the series

Mignon, Act II, with Philine in her Titania costume and Brian Ralph as Laërte-Oberon. Huguette Tourangeau sang Mignon

As the Daughter of the Regiment, with the puppets. From the television show *Who's Afraid of Opera?*

Enacting Offenbach's *La Perichole*. I adored playing this touchingly comic rôle. This, too, was in the television series

Backstage at the Bing Farewell Gala in 1972 with Lucine Amara, Teresa Zylis-Gara, and Pilar Lorengar

With Grace Bumbry backstage at the Met in 1972. We are both wearing gowns designed by Heinz Riva in Rome. Richard had conducted *Orfeo* at the Met with Grace

At the Gala on 22 April, 1972, to celebrate Rudolf Bing's farewell as General Manager of the Metropolitan Opera in New York. Here we are backstage with Montserrat Caballe and Placido Domingo. I sang the duo 'Sulla Tomba' from *Lucia di Lammermoor* with Luciano Pavarotti

Ljuba Welitsch played the Duchess of Krakenthorp at the Metropolitan Opera in 1972. She entered at the top of a staircase and stood there until the audience applauded. If the applause didn't come, she curtsied to the ground. The applause always came. Dramatic credibility went out of the window, but this grand old star whom I remember as a wonderful Salome, Tosca, and Lisa (in Tchaikovsky's *Queen of Spades*) deserved all her plaudits

Norma, Act I, San Francisco 1972

Regina Resnik as the Marquise de Berkenfield in the Metropolitan's *The Daughter of the Regiment* in 1972. This grand singer and actress is one of the few singers I know who have had a career for forty years and survived singing both Aida and Amneris, Gioconda and Laura, Amelia and Ulrica! She began as a soprano and is now a basso profundo. A wonderful, stimulating lady

Left: With Huguette Tourangeau in Tito Capobianco's production of Handel's *Rodelinda* designed by José Varona for the Netherlands Opera in 1973. Huguette had her best rôle as King Bertarido in this opera and gave a deeply moving performance **Right:** Richard and Huguette at our home in Les Avants

This picture gives some idea of the splendour of José Varona's magnificent costumes for the production of *Rodelinda* in Amsterdam

Jennie Tourel as the Duchess of Krakenthorp in the Chicago production of *The Daughter of the Regiment* in 1973. This is perhaps the last photo taken of her on stage as she died very soon afterwards

Ragnar Ulfung gave a truly comic performance as Alfred to my Rosalinde in San Francisco, 1973

Die Fledermaus, Act III, San Francisco, 1973.
Walter Slezak was an endearing and amusing
Frosch but his ad-libs made each performance a
little longer

Left: The wronged wife Act III **Right:** The Hungarian Countess in Act II with Nolan van Way as
Eisenstein. The production was by Lotfi Mansouri

As Antonia at the Metropolitan Opera with Placido Domingo as Hoffmann, 1973

As Giulietta in the Australian Opera's *The Tales of Hoffmann* with Henri Wilden in the title rôle, 1974

As Olympia in the Metropolitan Opera's *The Tales of Hoffmann* directed by Bliss Herbert and designed by Allen Klein, 1973. José Varona designed my costumes. Andrea Velis is Cochenille

Antonia in the Australian Opera's *The Tales of Hoffmann* directed by Tito Capobianco and designed by José Varona. This was our first return to our homeland since the great tour in 1965

Left: I first sang Massenet's *Esclarmonde* in San Francisco in 1974, with Giacomo Aragall as the knight Roland. The production was brilliantly conceived by Lotfi Mansouri. The fairy-tale designs were made by Beni Montrésor and my costumes by Barbara Matera **Right:** Once again with Giacomo Aragall. Also in the cast were Huguette Tourangeau as Parséis and Clifford Grant as the Emperor Phorcas. I spend half of the opera veiled

A photo taken in Vancouver *circa* 1976

With Her Royal Highness, the Duchess of Kent, and film star Roger Moore, 1975

I am vastly amused at a remark of Prince Charles but Sir John Tooley seems elsewhere. Taken in the Crush Bar at Covent Garden after the Darwin Relief Concert in January 1975. We were joined by Heather Begg, Margreta Elkins, Graham Clark, Clifford Grant, Tom McDonnell and Louis Quilico and the Royal Philharmonic Orchestra. The proceeds went to the victims of the fearful cyclone which practically demolished the city of Darwin on New Year's Eve, 1974

With Alfredo Kraus in Act I of the updated
Visconti production of *La Traviata* at Covent
Garden, 1975. I had also sung it with Alfredo at
the Teatro San Carlos in Lisbon in 1974

Left: *La Traviata*, Act IV **Right:** I actually appeared on a postage stamp published in Nicaragua in 1975.
Melba had to wait until she was dead!

Act III of *Il Trovatore*, San Francisco 1975.
Barbara Matera copied this costume from one
worn by Mlle George in a long forgotten drama

Luciano Pavarotti and I both made our *Il Trovatore* débuts in San Francisco in September 1975. Elena
Obrazova and Shirley Verrett both sang Azucena

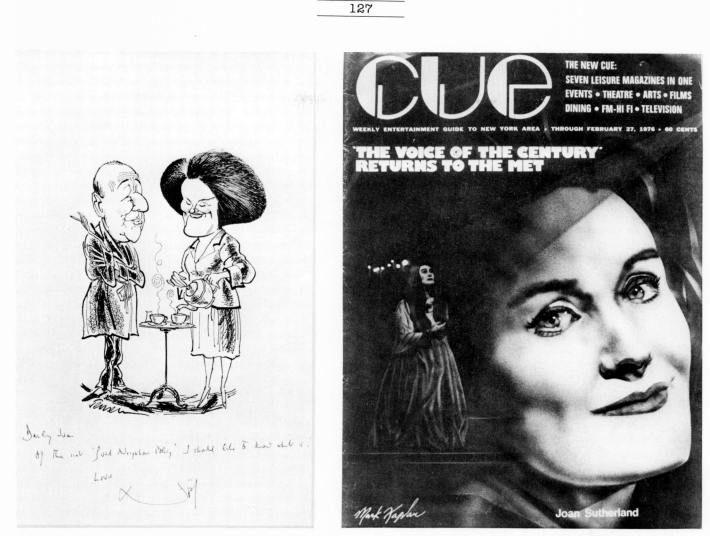

Left: This cartoon, 'Good Neighbours', by John Jensen of Sir Noël Coward and myself, appeared in one of the English newspapers *circa* 1975. Noël sent me a copy **Right:** Cover of *Cue* magazine, New York, 1976

Left: Another favourite record cover. The statue was commissioned by *Decca* as a promotional gimmick and has become a collector's item **Right:** Adam in the garden at Les Avants with Richard's god-daughter, Rachel, *circa* 1976

In *I Puritani* in 1976 Luciano Pavarotti and I caused our biggest sensation at the Metropolitan Opera in New York. The production was by Sandro Sequi, sets by Ming Cho Lee, and costumes by Peter J. Hall

Left: *The Merry Widow*, Act II, Vancouver, 1976. The production was by Lotfi Mansouri and the designs by José Varona **Right:** Act II, with Pieter van der Stolk as Danilo

A curtain call after *Esclarmonde* at the Metropolitan Opera, 1976, with John Carpenter as Enéas, Huguette Tourangeau as Parséis, and Jerome Hines as Phorcas

Left: We did a concert tour in New Zealand in 1976 and this photo was taken at the first concert in Wellington, on 19 May 1976 — which was televised **Right:** A cake arrives in my dressing room at Covent Garden during *Maria Stuarda* in 1977

Our good friends Gerry and Buddy Kaufman gave me a party for my fiftieth birthday in November, 1976. In the front row L — R are Gerry, Arthur Matera, Ania Dorfmann, Joanne Morris, Huguette Tourangeau, Barbara Matera, and in the back row L — R are James Morris, Martin Waldron, Bliss Johnston, Buddy, Ann Colbert, Martin Scheepers, and Norman Ayrton

The last scene of *Maria Stuarda* at Covent Garden in 1977. The production was by John Copley. Heather Begg (on the left) is Anna and Stuart Burrows (kneeeling) is Leicester

The Confessional, my favourite scene in *Maria Stuarda*, at Covent Garden in 1977. David Ward, who was a fellow student at the Royal College of Music in 1951, is Talbot

Richard with Her Majesty the Queen Mother and Sir John Tooley in the Crush Bar at Covent Garden after the *Maria Stuarda* Gala, 1977

Left: As Sita in Massenet's *Le Roi de Lahore*, Vancouver 1977. Toscanini conducted this opera in Ravenna in 1894 and at La Scala in 1899 **Right:** With Ron Stevens as Alim in the same Vancouver production

Le Roi de Lahore was Massenet's first major success and was a popular opera in France and Italy at the end of the 19th century. It was last heard at the Metropolitan Opera in 1926 (with Gigli) until we revived it in Vancouver and Seattle in 1977. The rôle of Sita is extremely dramatic and rewarding

Rosina Raisbeck as the Princess in the Australian Opera's *Suor Angelica*, 1977. Rosina's strong spine-chilling performance helped me enormously. I loved singing *Suor Angelica*, which was my first Puccini rôle on the professional stage

The same production of *Suor Angelica*. We later recorded the opera with Christa Ludwig as the Princess, Isobel Buchanan as Genovieffa, and Elizabeth Connell as the Monitress

Left: Cover of the Australian magazine *Hi-Fi and Music*, July 1978 **Right:** With Richard's mother and Adam on his 21st birthday in front of my portrait by Adelaide artist Robert Hannaford, painted in 1976

As *Norma* in Holland, 1978. This is one of my most performed rôles. In 1970 alone I sang in over thirty performances

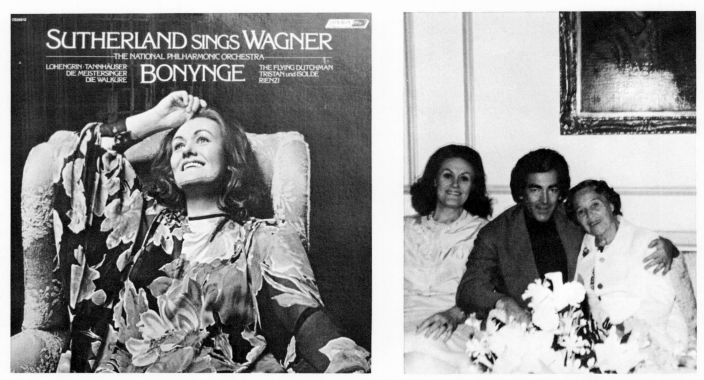

Left: One of my favourite record covers *circa* 1978 **Right:** We grew up with Annie Frind's recording of 'The Nun's Chorus' from *Casanova* and what joy when we met and became friends in the 1960s. She sang leading rôles with the Berlin State Opera under Leo Blech and in Dresden in the 1920s before her long successful runs in operetta. She generously gave us her wonderful collection of music, which we treasure. Here we are at the Ponchartrain Hotel in New Orleans in 1978

Left: Risë Stevens was a great Carmen, Mignon, and Delilah before our time at the Metropolitan. To see this glamorous lady today you might think it was only yesterday. Here we are in 1978 at the Manhattan School of Music, where we talked with the students **Right:** Dame Margot Fonteyn during a visit to Sydney in July 1978

The Merry Widow, Act III, at the Australian Opera
in Sydney, 1978, with Ron Stevens as Danilo. The
production was designed by Kristian Fredrikson
and directed by Lotfi Mansouri

Left: Cartoon by Moir of Sir Robert Helpmann and me **Right:** The jazz group Galapagos Duck paid a visit
to *Norma* in Sydney during 1978 and popped backstage to say hello with their manager Peter Brendle
(left) who is the brother of our housekeeper Ruthli, with us for thirty years!

Left: A bunch of tickets for a recital in Korea, 1978 **Right:** On a recital tour in Japan in 1978. I had previously sung Violetta in *La Traviata* in Tokyo and Osaka with the Metropolitan Opera in 1975

A curtain call after *Don Giovanni* at the Metropolitan Opera in 1978, with James Morris as the Don. The opera was given in the old but still beautiful sets of Eugene Berman. My costume was copied by Barbara Matera from a dress worn by Louis XIV's Queen, Marie-Thérèse. I naughtily wore it on television as the Court dress in the second act of Offenbach's *La Périchole*

At the Inaugural Gala Concert for the Australian Music Foundation which we gave at Covent Garden with HRH the Prince of Wales and Dame Edna Everage, alias Barry Humphries

Left: Zinka Milanov has given us some of our greatest evenings in the theatre and some superb advice out of it. A great singer, a great cook, and a sharp conversationalist — an evening spent in her company is one to remember. Here she is in her New York apartment in front of a painting of herself as Tosca **Right:** I was laid up with a cold during a run of *La Traviata* in Melbourne in 1979. Michael Stennett painted this picture to cheer me up

I sang my first Elektra for the Australian Opera when *Idomeneo* was given for the first time in 1979 in a production by Robin Lovejoy, designed by John Truscott. The cast was very strong, with Leona Mitchell in an ideal rôle as Ilia and Margreta Elkins as Idamante. Ron Stevens and later Serge Baigildin sang Idomeneo

As Elektra singing the aria 'D' Oreste, d' Ajace', Australian Opera, 1979

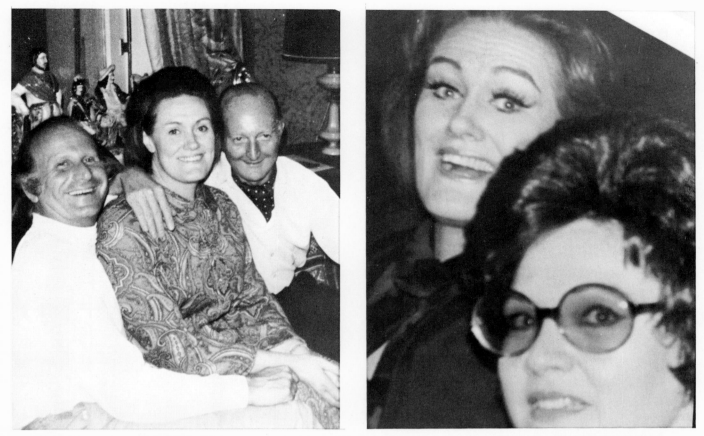

Left: In Les Avants with Norman Ayrton (left) and Douglas Gamley, *circa* 1980. Douglas and Richard revamped *The Beggar's Opera*, which was performed by the Australian Opera in 1981 and recorded for Decca. Apart from having written a mere forty or so film scores, Douglas has done many orchestral arrangements for my recordings **Right:** A casual snap with Jackie (Marilyn Horne)

Chatting backstage with HRH Prince Charles during a rehearsal for *Lucrezia Borgia* at Covent Garden, 1980

Upper left: Covent Garden mounted *Lucrezia Borgia* in March 1980. Sir John Tooley had just presented me with the Royal Opera House commemorative silver medal for long service (28 years) **Lower left:** Rehearsing at Covent Garden for *Lucrezia Borgia* with John Copley and Alfredo Kraus **Right:** *Lucrezia Borgia* programme cover

Alfredo Kraus sang the rôle of Gennaro. *Lucrezia Borgia* was produced by John Copley, with sets by John Pascoe and costumes by Michael Stennett — a very handsome and romantic production

Michael Stennett painted this extravaganza for us in our music room at Les Avants. Besides me in many rôles, the picture contains a multitude of souvenirs!

Left: The New Zealand and Australian wicket-keepers, Warren Lees and Rodney Marsh came to an Adelaide performance of *Lucia* in 1980 and presented me with a World Series Cup cricket bat signed by the New Zealand team for our son Adam, who is a great cricket fan **Right:** We spent a lovely evening with Kiri Te Kanawa and her husband, Des Park, in London, *circa* 1981

With our indispensible wig mistress, Shirley
Germain, getting ready for Act I of the Australian
Opera's *I Masnadieri* in 1980. We recorded the
opera in 1982 with Franco Bonisolli, Matteo
Manuguerra, and Samuel Ramey

Left: A curtain call after Act I of *Lucrezia Borgia*, Rome Opera, 1980 **Right:** In Sydney, Act II of
I Masnadieri, singing the aria 'Tu del mio Carlo al seno' at the tomb of Massimiliano. This production was by
Peter Beauvais and designed by Allan Lees, with costumes by Michael Stennett

When I was made a Doctor of Laws at the Australian National University in 1980, the *Canberra Times* referred to me as Dame Margaret Sutherland (we have a composer of the same name). Michael Stennett commemorated the event

Regina Resnik as Prince Orlovsky in our 1980 *Fledermaus* in San Diego

With Beverly Sills in the Finale of Tito Capobianco's production of *Die Fledermaus* in San Diego, 1980. I sang Rosalinde and Beverly, Adele. We made such a good comedy pair we should have teamed up together. It was also fun working with Alan Titus (Eisenstein) and Giuseppe Campora (Alfred)

Beverly gave a birthday dinner to celebrate Richard's fiftieth in 1980. In the picture L-R: Alan Titus, Spiro Malas (Frank), Beverly, Gigi and Tito Capobianco, Regina Resnik

Richard with Angela Lansbury and Kiri Te Kanawa listening to a play-back during the recording of *The Beggar's Opera* in Kingsway Hall, London, 1981. Kiri and I were rather terrified of our dialogues with Angela, and Angela was petrified at having to sing with the opera stars. We had a lot of fun making this recording

Left: *Norma* Act III in Toronto, 1981. Here I am about to kill the children. The production was directed by Lotfi Mansouri and designed by José Varona. It was seen on Canadian television **Right:** Also in Toronto, with Tatiana Troyanos as Adalgisa. I have sung in *Norma* with many marvellous Adalgisas including Marilyn Horne, Fiorenza Cossotto (at the Teatro Colon, Buenos Aires), Huguette Tourangeau, Margreta Elkins, Heather Begg, and Doris Soffel (most recently in Stockholm, 1985, and Barcelona, 1986)

I sang Desdemona in Sydney in 1981, 22 years after my last performance in Vienna in 1959. Heather Begg was Emilia; Angelo Marenzi, Otello; and John Shaw, Iago. Production by George Ogilvie, sets by Shaun Gurton, costumes by Kristian Fredrikson, and the conductor Carlo Felice Cillario

Left: With Carlo Felice Cillario in Sydney, 1981. He conducted a glorious *Otello* **Right:** Richard with Rita Hunter, 1981. Rita now lives in Sydney and sings regularly with the Australian Opera

Left: In the Visconti production of *Il Trovatore* with Franco Bonisolli, Covent Garden 1981. Elena Obrazova was Azucena **Right:** On 20 and 23 March 1981, we gave a Gala Concert in Avery Fisher Hall, New York City, with Marilyn Horne and Luciano Pavarotti

Left: *La Traviata*, Act I, Australian Opera, 1981 **Right:** Act III of the same opera. This production was by John Copley, with sets by Henry Bardon and costumes by Michael Stennett

Left: As Queen Marguerite de Valois, in Act III of *Les Huguenots*, Australian Opera, 1981. Anson Austin as Raoul stands behind me. The production is by Lotfi Mansouri with sets by John Stoddart and costumes by Michael Stennett. **Right:** This nonsense poster was produced by Peter Davies after our *Huguenots* performance (the Opera House stands on Bennelong Point)

Act II of *Les Huguenots*, with Marilyn Zschau as Valentine

In 1981 we took part in a recording produced by the *Sydney Morning Herald*, 'Australian Musical Heritage,' to commemorate the 150th anniversary of Sydney's oldest newspaper. The proceeds went to the Royal Alexandra Hospital for Children

Above: Act II of *The Merry Widow* in San Francisco, 1981, with Håkan Hagegård as Danilo. I adore the Widow; I can laugh and stay alive at the end **Right:** With Lotfi Mansouri, whose 1981 production of *The Merry Widow* was stunning

Richard at supper with Marilyn Horne in San Rafael, 1981, when they were performing *Semiramide* in San Francisco with Montserrat Caballé in the title rôle

Left: Cover, *Opera News*, 1982 **Right:** Michael Stennett painted this *Merry Widow* portrait in 1982

Her Majesty, Queen Elizabeth the Queen Mother presented both the Prince of Wales and me with honorary Doctorates of Music at the Royal College of Music, 1982

Adam and his wife Helen spend most weekends at the beach with us when we are in Sydney (February 1982)

I visit the boys of St Andrews Cathedral School, Sydney, 1982

OMAGGIO A VENEZIA
JOAN SUTHERLAND
«dedicato a MARIA MALIBRAN»
TEATRO MALIBRAN
9 APRILE 1982 ORE 21

Joan Sutherland ritratta da Arbit Blatas

Left: We did a recital in the lovely old Teatro Malibran in Venice in 1982. Arbit Blatas, who had seen me in *Die Fledermaus*, painted this portrait from memory for the occasion **Right:** Of all the singers we have ever known, Renata Tebaldi is the most beloved, not only because of her voice but because of her own personal loveliness. Her Mimis and Butterflys remain with us forever. This photograph was taken after a concert at the Teatro Malibran

Left: Venice, 1982 **Right:** At home, the same year

Left: As Rosalinde in Act I of *Die Fledermaus*, the Australian Opera, 1982. I so hated the dowdy costumes designed for me that I wore my old ones in Acts I and III **Right:** The Mad Scene in *Lucia* at the Metropolitan Opera in 1982. Alfredo Kraus was Edgardo, and the opera was televised

Homage from the Prime Minister to the Prima Donna. Mr Bob Hawke backstage after *Il Trovatore* in Sydney, 1983

Left: *Alcina* — the Australian Opera's sumptuous 1983 production directed by Sir Robert Helpmann and designed by John Pascoe. My costumes were by Barbara Matera. **Right:** In *Alcina* Margreta Elkins again sang Ruggiero, as she had done in the Covent Garden production in 1962. We also sang the opera together in Carnegie Hall in 1965

Taken in the artists' room at Kingsway Hall, London, during the recording of *Hamlet* in 1983. L-R are Sherrill Milnes (Hamlet), John Tomlinson (the Ghost), Sylvia Holford (répétiteur), Gösta Winbergh (Laërte) and Barbara Conrad (the Queen)

'Big P' and I prepare for a dive. I affectionately christened Luciano with this nickname several years ago and we were amused to see a recent recording appear in Italy under the same title.

Cartoon by Aragon, 1983

Leonie Rysanek is one of the great ladies of the operatic world. I sang with her in *Die Walküre* in 1955 and *Elektra* back in 1954, and in 1983 Leonie sang the aria from Lehar's *Giuditta* during a Sydney *Fledermaus*, when I sang Rosalinde. Leonie has just had a triumphant Gala celebrating her twenty-five years at the Metropolitan Opera and is at the top of her form

We gave a Gala concert in the Concert Hall of the Sydney Opera House on 23 January 1983, with Luciano Pavarotti. The concert was televised and released on video cassette. Between Richard and myself is the concertmaster, Ladislav Jasek

Adam and Helen's wedding at St John's Church, Darlinghurst, Sydney, January 1982

The Australian artist Judy Cassab painted me as Lakmé. This painting hangs in the Sydney Opera House

Above: This cartoon of Luciano Pavarotti and ourselves by Colquhoun appeared in the Sydney *Sunday Telegraph* on 6 February 1983, during his visit to Sydney **Below:** There was some doubt as to whether Luciano Pavarotti would appear in Sydney as he suddenly announced he was allergic to stage dust. Colquhoun made this comment in the *Sydney Morning Herald* (January 1983)

With Luciano Pavarotti during his visit to Sydney in 1982

Luciano Pavarotti with Chester (our 'do-all') and Richard at our beach house outside Sydney, February 1983

This was our first sight of our grand-daughter at Sydney airport in June 1983. Natasha Katarina was born on May 4. I think her parents had been on a diet of Russian novels

I sang 'Mira o Norma' with Margreta Elkins at a concert in Sydney to benefit victims of the Victorian bushfires in February 1983

Anyone for tennis? 1983

Semiramide at the Australian Opera, 1983

Left: *The Daughter of the Regiment*, Metropolitan Opera 1983, with Alfredo Kraus. This original Covent Garden production was bought by the Metropolitan Opera and 'loaned' in turn to Vancouver and Chicago
Right: I first sang Cilea's *Adriana Lecouvreur* in San Diego in 1983. The production was by Tito Capobianco. Vasile Moldoveanu sang Maurizio; Stella Silva, the Princess; and John Broechler, Michonnet

At a party at Gigi and Tito Capobianco's with Stella
Silva who sang the Princesse de Bouillon with me
in *Adriana Lecouvreur* in San Diego in 1983

Esclarmonde, Covent Garden 1983

This is our latest studio photograph together, taken in Sydney in January 1983

Taken in our garden in April 1984 after some very late snow

Act I of *Adriana Lecouvreur*. The Australian Opera production directed by John Copley and designed by Alan Lees with costumes by Michael Stennett, 1984

Adriana recites the monologue from Racine's *Phedre* in Act III *Adriana Lecouvreur*, Australian Opera 1984. Anson Austin sang Maurizio; Heather Begg, the Princess; and John Shaw, Michonnet

Left: We took the Canadian Opera production of *Anna Bolena* to Detroit (June 1984), San Francisco (October 1984) and Chicago (October 1985). Performances are scheduled for Houston in 1986 **Below:** *Anna Bolena*, Act I – the magnificent production made for me by the Canadian Opera in May 1984. The sumptuous sets and costumes were by John Pascoe and Michael Stennett and the production by Lotfi Mansouri. James Morris sang Henry VIII; Judith Forst, Jane Seymour; and Michael Myers, Percy

Anna Bolena is my latest Donizetti rôle and the biggest challenge of all his many heroines that I have sung

Taken backstage with Horst Hoffmann during *The Tales of Hoffmann* (no relation!) at the Australian Opera, 1984, with our grand-daughter Natasha

The Order of Australia was presented to Richard on 24 February 1984, which was the occasion of this family portrait. My mother-in-law is on the left and Richard's aunt next to me

Not another singer in the family! Natasha sat through Act III of *Adriana Lecouvreur* and sang along, aged eight months, (January 1984)

I Masnadieri, San Diego 1984

As the New Prioress in the Australian Opera's production in 1984, twenty-six years since I last sang the rôle.

Montserrat Caballé has just made a wicked remark to me during our *Norma* recording in London, 1984

Backstage during an open-air concert performance of *The Tales of Hoffmann*, Sydney 1985

Act IV, *Norma*, Australian Opera, 1985

'Mad Scene', *Lucia*, Covent Garden 1985

Taking my applause after the 'Mad Scene', *Lucia*,
Covent Garden 1985

The cast of *Rodelinda*, which we recorded in London, April 1985. L-R Alicia Nafe, Curtis Rayam, Huguette Tourangeau, Samuel Ramey and Isobel Buchanan

The latest addition to our family — Vanya Nicholas, born 14 August 1985

As Ophelia in *Hamlet*, Toronto 1985. Lotfi Mansouri directed, and the costumes were by Michael Stennett

My most recent Lucia, at the Australian Opera in Sydney, February 1986

Michael Stennett has designed several of my most notable costumes. This one was for Act I of *Anna Bolena* in the Canadian Opera production, Toronto 1984

ANNOUNCING A VERY SPECIAL PUBLISHING EVENT . . .

JOAN SUTHERLAND

DESIGNS FOR A PRIMA DONNA

RICHARD BONYNGE

·THE CRAFTSMAN'S PRESS·

July 1985 saw the publication of Richard's first book — a sumptuous limited edition restricted to 500 copies. Titled *Joan Sutherland: Designs for a Prima Donna*, it was published by Sydney art-book company The Craftsman's Press and featured designs by Franco Zeffirelli, Michael Stennett, José Varona, John Piper, Kristian Fredrikson and Desmond Digby — among many others.

In March 1986 Richard and I performed in Wellington, New Zealand. We gave two concerts and a recital. This photograph was taken at the time of the first concert

It was lovely of Luciano Pavarotti to send us the tribute which appears at the front of this album. Luciano very much enjoys swimming and this shot was taken beside our pool during his last visit to Sydney in the summer of 1983. It seems appropriate to end the album with a photograph where we all have the last laugh together!

ACKNOWLEDGEMENTS

Collection of Dame Joan Sutherland and Richard Bonynge: 14; 15; 16; 17; 19; 20; 21 (lower); 22 (upper); 24 (upper right); 25 (upper and lower left); 26 (upper); 27; 28 (lower); 29; 31 (lower left); 32 (upper and lower left); 34 (middle); 35 (lower); 36 (upper left and right); 37 (upper); 40 (upper); 42 (upper); 44 (upper); 45 (lower); 46 (upper right); 48 (lower left); 49 (upper left); 56 (upper); 57 (upper left); 58; 60 (lower); 68 (upper right); 71 (lower); 74 (lower right); 75 (lower); 76; 79; 80 (upper); 81; 82 (lower left and lower right); 84 (lower); 85; 87 (upper and lower left); 88 (lower); 89 (upper right and lower left); 90 (upper left and right); 92 (upper left); 95 (lower); 96 (upper right and lower); 97 (lower); 99 (upper and lower left);100 (lower left); 101 (upper); 104 (upper left); 105 (upper left); 106 (upper right); 108 (lower); 109; 110 (upper right); 111 (upper right); 112 (upper right); 114; 115; 116; 117 (upper right); 118 (upper); 124 (upper); 126 (upper); 127 (lower right); 129; 130 (upper right); 134; 135 (upper right and lower); 136 (upper right and lower left and right); 137 (upper and lower right); 138 (upper right and lower); 139 (lower left); 141 (upper left and right); 143 (lower left); 144 (lower left); 148 (upper and lower left); 152 (upper left); 157 (lower); 160; 161; 162 (lower); 163 (upper); 166 (upper); 170 (lower); 174; 182

Lee Photo Studio: 18 (lower); Covent Garden Archives: 21 (upper right); 24 (lower); 26 (lower); 32 (lower right); 52 (lower); Pearl Freeman: 21 (upper left); Roger Wood: 21 (lower); Helga Sharland: 23 (upper left and lower); Angus McBean: 23 (upper right); 80 (lower); 94 (lower right); Denis de Marney: 24 (upper left); 28 (upper left); Derek Allan: 25 (lower right); 33 (upper); Star Studio: 28 (upper right); Roy Hobdell: 30 (upper); 44 (upper); A. Dawson: 30 (lower); Houston Rogers: 31 (upper); 33 (lower left and right); 39 (upper right and left); 41; 51 (lower); 65; 77; 78; 92 (upper right); 93 (upper right); Guy Gravett; 31 (lower right); Svarre/Cantion: 34 (upper and lower); Reynolds News: 35 (upper); 37 (lower); London News Agency: 36 (lower); 40 (lower); Covent Garden Books: 38 (upper); David Sim: 38 (lower); Fayer: 39; 49 (lower left); Giusto Scafidi: 39 (lower right); 45 (upper); 47 (lower right); 48 (upper); 59 (upper left and right); *The Observer*: 42 (lower); *Radio Times*: 43 (upper); Publifoto: 46 (upper left and lower); *Sydney Morning Herald*: 47 (upper); 151; La Fenice Archives: 47 (lower left); Agence de Presse Bernard: 48 (lower right); Michel Petit: 49 (upper right); Decca Record Company: 51 (upper); 94 (upper left and right); 101 (lower left and right); 110 (upper left); *New York Times*: 53 (lower right); RAS Barcelona: 52 (upper); 66 (upper); Franco Zeffirelli: 53 (upper); Lillo Foto: 53 (lower left); E. Piccagliani: 54 (upper left); 55 (lower left and right); 56 (lower); 62; 64; La Scala Archives: 54 (upper right); 67; Foto Italia: 54 (lower); *Vita*: 55 (upper); United Press International: 57 (upper right); 139 (upper); D. Straughan: 57 (lower); Eleanor Morrison: 59 (lower); 60 (upper); 68 (lower); 71 (upper); 94 (lower left); Nicholas Treatt: 61 (upper); Anthony Crickmay: 63 (upper); 93 (lower left); 125 (lower); Foto Troncone: 63 (lower); Forabola: 64 (upper); Gran Teatro del Liceo Archives: 66 (lower); Anne Roughley: 68 (upper left); Chester Carone: 69 (upper left); 84 (upper); 100 (upper right); 110 (lower); 130 (lower); 143 (lower right); 146 (lower); 148 (lower right); 152 (lower); 154 (upper); 158 (upper); 164 (lower); 168 (upper); 172 (lower); 188-9; Whiteston Photo: 69 (lower); *Newsweek*: 71; Sedge Le Blang: 72 (upper); *Life*: 72 (lower); 104 (lower); Barry Glass: 73 (lower); 98; Arthur Todd: 74 (upper); Louise Melancon: 74 (lower left); 120; 121 (lower); Beth Bergman: 75 (upper); 128; O. Fernandez: 82 (upper); Hans Beacham: 83 (upper left); John Pineda: 83 (upper right); Jorgen Schytte/ Delta: 83 (lower); Allan Studios: 86; 88 (upper); Cameo Photos: 87 (lower right); *The Australian Women's Weekly*: 88 (upper left); 149 (lower left); 172 (upper); Tony Rafty: 89 (lower right); Rigby: 90 (lower); Cole Leslie: 91 (upper); Nicke Luciani: 91 (lower); *Daily Express*: 92 (lower); Donald Southern: 93 (upper left); 96 (upper left); 132 (upper); Reg Wilson: 93 (lower right); 95 (upper right); 131; 142 (upper left and lower); 149 (upper left); 166 (lower); Dennis Galloway: 95 (upper left); Gretl Geiger: 97 (upper); Foto Marchiori: 99 (lower right); Du Vinage: 102 (upper); Elisabeth Speidel: 102 (lower left and right); 107 (upper left and lower); 108 (upper); Alfa/Teatro Colon: 103 (upper left and right); *Evening Standard*: 103 (lower); Louis Peres: 104 (upper right); 149 (upper left); Max Waldman: 105 (upper right); José Varona: 106 (upper left); Adrian Siegel: 106 (lower); Foto Lieske: 107 (upper left); Rainer Stern: 111 (upper left); Kroll Productions: 111 (lower); 112 (upper left and lower); 113; Maria Austria: 117 (upper left and lower); Carolyn Mason Jones: 118 (lower); 119 (lower left and right); 122 (lower left and right); San Francisco Opera Archives: 119 (upper); John C. Walsh: 121 (upper); 122 (upper); Tony Hauser: 123; *Daily Telegraph*: 124 (lower); Stuart Robinson: 125 (upper); Ron Scherl: 126 (lower); John Jensen: 127 (upper left); *Cue* magazine: 127 (upper right); London Record Company: 127 (lower left); 136 (upper right); Television One, New Zealand: 130 (upper left); Philip Clement: 132 (lower left and right); 133; 147 (lower right); *Hi-Fi and Music* magazine: 135 (upper left); Moir: 137 (lower left); Michael Stennett: 139 (lower right); 142 (upper right); 143 (upper); 145 (upper); 153 (upper); 185; Branco Gaica: 140; 144 (upper and lower right); 149 (lower right); 150 (upper left and lower); 156 (upper left); 157 (upper left and right); 159 (upper); 165 (upper); 168 (lower); 169; 175; 177; 178; Tony Auguste: 141 (lower); Clive Boursnell: 142 (mid-left); San Diego Opera Archives: 145 (lower); 146 (upper); Clive Barda: 147 (upper); 179; 180-1; Robert C. Ragsdale: 147 (lower); 183; Anson Austin: 150 (upper right); Ira Nowinski: 152 (upper right); *Opera News*: 153 (upper left); Foto Attualita: 155 (upper right and lower left); James Heffernan: 156 (upper right); 165 (lower left); John Fairfax & Sons: 156 (lower); 159 (lower); Aragon: 158 (lower); Colquhoun/*Sunday Telegraph*: 162 (upper); *Sun Herald*: 163 (lower); News Ltd.: 164 (upper); Jan Dryden: 165 (lower right); Patrick Jones: 167; Robert Cahen: 170 (upper); 171; *The Australian*: 173; Malcolm Crowthers: 176; 180-81; Paul Richardson: 184; Jocelyn Corlin: 187